AF228975

BECOME AN
AIRCRAFT MECHANIC

by Mike Downs

BrightPoint Press

San Diego, CA

© 2025 BrightPoint Press
an imprint of ReferencePoint Press, Inc.
Printed in the United States

For more information, contact:
BrightPoint Press
PO Box 27779
San Diego, CA 92198
www.BrightPointPress.com

LIBRARY OF CONGRESS CATALOGING-IN-PUBLICATION DATA

Names: Downs, Mike, author.
Title: Become an aircraft mechanic / by Mike Downs.
Description: San Diego, CA: BrightPoint Press, [2025] | Series: Skilled and vocational trades | Includes bibliographical references and index. | Audience: Grades 7-9
Identifiers: LCCN 2024004123 (print) | LCCN 2024004124 (eBook) | ISBN 9781678209025 (hardcover) | ISBN 9781678209032 (eBook)
Subjects: LCSH: Airplanes--Maintenance and repair--Vocational guidance--Juvenile literature.
Classification: LCC TL671.9.D69 2025 (print) | LCC TL671.9 (eBook) | DDC 629.134/6--dc23/eng/20240207
LC record available at https://lccn.loc.gov/2024004123
LC eBook record available at https://lccn.loc.gov/2024004124

CONTENTS

- Aircraft mechanics work on many kinds of aircraft. They can work on gliders, propeller airplanes, helicopters, drones, and jets.

- Aircraft mechanics might work for large airlines, special repair stations, or small aircraft operators.

- Aircraft mechanics learn basic welding, fabric stitching, piston engine repair, and jet engine repair.

- Some aircraft mechanics work mostly on avionics. These systems include radar, radios, navigation equipment, and autopilots.

- Aircraft mechanics might specialize in avionics, balloons, airships, rotorcraft, or unmanned aircraft systems (UAS). An unmanned aircraft system includes a drone, the system that controls it, and the operator.

- Most aircraft mechanics are Airframe and Powerplant (A&P) mechanics. This means they work on aircraft and their engines.

- Aircraft mechanics who become managers might develop safety procedures or policies for a company.

- An aircraft mechanic earns much higher pay than the average worker.

- Aircraft mechanics are needed everywhere. Some airlines have programs to help pay for aircraft mechanic training.

AN IMPORTANT JOB

Elena Gonzalez walked into the aircraft **hangar**. A Boeing 737 aircraft sat waiting for her. It needed work. Gonzalez picked up her work card. This is a form that explains what needs to be fixed. The air conditioning system wasn't working properly. This air conditioner had already broken twice. It had stopped working when the airplane was flying. Gonzalez's job was to find out why.

Aircraft mechanics use platforms and ladders to make repairs to parts that are hard to reach.

Gonzalez checked the maintenance computer. Mechanics always make a note in the computer whenever they work on an airplane. She looked up what other aircraft mechanics had done to try to fix it. Figuring it out wouldn't be easy. But Gonzalez liked solving problems.

Airliner jets have computers that send codes when something is broken. These codes help mechanics find the problem. But sometimes the information isn't exact. And there can be more than one code. Gonzalez decided to replace a part in the air conditioner called the actuator. This is a small motor that moves the vent doors. When these doors open, cool air flows into the airplane's cabin. She tested the air conditioner and it worked. But the air conditioner also had to work when the airplane was in the air.

Early the next morning, the plane took off. The air conditioner worked perfectly.

Before a plane leaves the runway, mechanics must verify that any recent issues entered into the maintenance computer log have been resolved.

Gonzalez had made a difference. "There is nothing more rewarding than fixing an airplane," says Gonzalez, "and then watching it fly away."[1]

WHAT IS AN AIRCRAFT MECHANIC?

Aircraft mechanics have an important job. They fix anything that is broken on an aircraft. They work on big components. These include jet engines, wings, and brakes. Mechanics also fix things such as air conditioners, carpeting, and broken seats. And they inspect aircraft to make sure they are safe. Mechanics maintain aircraft to keep them in good shape.

Aircraft mechanics work for big companies such as airlines. They work

Aircraft mechanics may work on small private aircraft or big jets that fly for major airlines.

for medium-sized companies that fly a few airplanes. Some work for helicopter sightseeing tour companies. Others work at flight training schools and in the military. They are needed all around the world.

CHAPTER ONE

WHAT DOES AN AIRCRAFT MECHANIC DO?

Norman Mello has been an aircraft mechanic for many years. "Being an aircraft mechanic can be a fun job!" he says. A certified aircraft mechanic can fix all kinds of aircraft. "You are certified to work on small **antique aircraft**," he explained. "You are certified to work on big jets and fixed-wing and helicopters."[2]

Aircraft mechanics learn to fix all the parts of an aircraft. They can stitch fabric or

Some aircraft mechanics prefer to fix mainly older aircraft.

VALVRING OIL
(N.Z.) LTD
BETTER LUBRICATION WITH
Representing
VALVRING OIL CORP.
PHONE 86.498
valvring
OIL
LOS ANGELES
MASTERTON N.Z.
CALIFORNIA U.S.A.
BLK

use their **welding** skills to repair aluminum. They change tires, replace propellers, and fix jet engines. Aircraft mechanics also work on wiring, instruments, and flight controls.

WORKING FOR AIRLINES

Many aircraft mechanics work for airlines. They make sure the airliners are safe to fly. When something breaks on an airplane, the pilot will report the problem using a radio. A mechanic will be ready when the airplane arrives at the gate. When the passenger door opens, the mechanic talks to the pilot. They will ask for the aircraft maintenance logbook. This is where pilots write down problems with the aircraft. The mechanic uses the pilot's notes to help fix the problem. For example, when the mechanic replaces an electronic part for the **radar**, they will add a note in the logbook that the radar is fixed. Then they add the work into a computer. Airlines use computers to track every problem.

Sometimes aircraft mechanics fix jet engine problems. After an engine is fixed,

Mechanics may work together to fix jet engines. Their goal is to get commercial flights back in the air safely as quickly as possible.

it must be checked. One aircraft mechanic
will start the engine. Another will watch
from the outside. They make sure it is
working correctly.

Aircraft mechanics can also move big
airliners. If a plane has been fixed in the
maintenance hangar, it needs to go to
the terminal. Aircraft mechanics hook up
a pushback tug to the front landing gear.
They use it to tow the airplane to the gate.

Computer Resets

Airliners use many computers. They have
computers to detect fire. Computers also operate
flight controls. Sometimes the computers stop
working. Mechanics shut off the entire airplane
to reset the computers. It's a little like restarting
a laptop.

A pushback tug makes it easier for mechanics to move big aircraft from the runway to the hangar.

Sometimes they don't have a tug. Then two aircraft mechanics will get into the cockpit. They will start the engines and taxi, or move, the airplane to a gate.

Aircraft mechanics also fix small problems. Sometimes a coffee maker is broken or the carpet in the aircraft is torn. Other times a seat won't recline or a bathroom faucet is leaking. An aircraft mechanic fixes all these things. When a new aircraft mechanic is hired, they learn from an experienced mechanic. They watch the mechanic work and make repairs. Each day they learn more about fixing aircraft.

OTHER JOBS

Aircraft mechanics do more than repair aircraft. Jason Yoder is an American Airlines **avionics** technical crew chief. He does C checks. These are overall checkups to make sure the plane is working well. A C check is done every 2 years. It includes testing pumps, actuators, and doors. Mechanics check the wings, fuselage, and tail for flaws in the metal. They remove the seats and fix anything that is broken. Yoder fixes everything. He makes sure the airplane is ready to go back into service.

Other mechanics do daily checks

on aircraft at the terminal gates.

Mechanics check the oil levels in

**Aircraft mechanics check the tires on planes during
routine inspections to make sure they are in good shape
to taxi, take off, and land.**

the engines. They check the airplane for any damage. They inspect the jet engines. They search for cracks or any other problems. They look at vents, tires, lights, and windows. They make sure the aircraft is safe and ready to fly. If everything is in order, the mechanics make a note in the maintenance computer that the airplane is safe.

Norman Mello develops safety and maintenance rules for his company. These rules keep pilots and passengers safe. He checks reports to see if there are any problems. And he talks to his mechanics about issues. Once he noticed that a **pressurization valve** was failing a lot. His mechanics kept replacing the part. He figured out it was a problem with

Mechanics follow a list of procedures to check and repair jet engines on aircraft.

Aircraft mechanics may work on spacecraft. They ensure that all systems are working before the rocket is cleared for liftoff.

the part. The safety and maintenance reports helped him solve the problem.

Aircraft mechanics can also work on some parts of spacecraft. They might check for leaks in the oxygen system. Or they might make sure the hatches are working properly. They can check the fuel tanks and capsules for cracks. They do tests to see whether systems are working. Many of these tasks are the same as for an airplane.

CHAPTER TWO

WHAT TRAINING DO AIRCRAFT MECHANICS NEED?

Training to become an aircraft mechanic is both fun and challenging. Most aircraft mechanic schools require a high school diploma. Math, reading, and computer skills are important for aircraft mechanics. They use math to measure an engine part to the thousandth of an inch. Reading is important to understand aircraft manuals and procedures.

Students learn how to fix aircraft with a lot of hands-on practice and guidance from experienced mechanics.

They use computers to track work and
diagnose problems.

The fastest track to becoming an aircraft
mechanic is aircraft mechanic school.
These programs take about 18 months.
Students learn basic aircraft systems. These
include air conditioning, engines, electrics,
and fuel. Students also learn the body of
an aircraft. This is called the airframe. It
might be made of fabric, metal, and other
materials. Students learn to inspect parts
of an aircraft. They make sure everything
is working properly. They learn to solve
problems. They keep track of what they do
in computers and on special forms.

Students do some training on computers.
Other training takes place in classrooms.
But much of the training is hands-on.

Mechanics must learn how to fix all parts of an airplane, including the wings.

Students learn how to fix all the parts of an aircraft. Many propeller airplanes have piston engines. Students learn how to fix these engines. They also work on jet engines, landing gear, and wings. They work on cockpits and flight controls as well.

A&P CERTIFICATE

Aircraft mechanic schools teach students the skills they need to work on many kinds

of airplanes. These skills will help them to
get their Airframe and Powerplant (A&P)
certificate. The powerplant is the engine.
An A&P certificate is a license to work
on aircraft.

Some mechanics prefer working on
airframes. Others like working on engines.
Fully qualified A&Ps are in high demand
for jobs. A&P Jason Yoder explains why.
"A&P certificated mechanics are the most

Different Names

A person who earns an A&P certificate is certified
as an Aviation Maintenance Technician (AMT)
by the Federal Aviation Administration (FAA).
They are also called an Aircraft Technician
(AT) or Aviation Maintenance Engineer (AME).
Sometimes they are simply called A&Ps.

versatile people you will meet," he says. "They have the training and experience to repair wood, metal, and advanced composite structures. There is nothing a true A&P cannot repair!"[3]

TESTING

Students must pass three written tests to get their A&P certificate. The first is the general knowledge test. It includes questions about safety, fire protection, and **aircraft servicing**. The second test is the airframe knowledge test. It tests students on fabric and metal repair, as well as on many aircraft flight systems. These include the fuel system and landing gear. The third test is the powerplant knowledge test. Students answer questions about jet

and piston engines, propellers, removing engines, and more.

To earn an A&P certificate, students must also pass the oral and practical exam. This hands-on exam takes 1 to 2 days. An FAA inspector oversees the exam. The FAA is responsible for certifying aircraft mechanics in the United States. The inspector will ask questions and watch the student work.

Students must demonstrate how to work on airframes. They might stitch fabric or weld aluminum. They demonstrate how to work on engines. They might also **troubleshoot** an engine problem on a real airplane. The FAA inspector will make sure the student knows how to work on

Learning to fix the outside of an aircraft is part of an aircraft mechanic's training. Students learn to weld and repair panels.

aircraft systems. Students are tested on everything they have learned.

Once students pass the oral and practical exam, the inspector will sign off on their certificate. This means they officially have their A&P license and can apply for jobs.

ANOTHER PATH

Going to an aircraft mechanic school is not required to get an A&P certificate. People who have worked in a similar job for at least 30 months can also take the tests. When they pass the oral, written, and practical exam, they can become a licensed A&P mechanic.

Some might first work as an assistant to an A&P mechanic. This is called an apprenticeship. They learn about airframes and powerplants on the job. Others might have experience rebuilding cars or other equipment. These skills are similar to those of an aircraft mechanic. If they can show they have worked for at least 30 months in these types of jobs, they can qualify to take all the exams. They may have to complete some additional training first.

Mechanics who have worked on cars or other engines for a certain amount of time can take the A&P exam.

CHAPTER THREE

WHAT IS LIFE LIKE AS AN AIRCRAFT MECHANIC?

Todd Wean works at Daytona Aircraft Services. This is an FAA-certified repair station. Wean works on anything from small propeller airplanes to midsize jets. He can install new equipment, fix aircraft problems, or do inspections.

"I start work about 8:30," says Wean, "and finish up at 5."[4] He normally arrives a bit early and chats with his fellow mechanics. They discuss the airplanes

Aircraft mechanics maintain and repair engines so that passenger jets can safely fly people to their destinations.

they are working on. They talk about any problems they might have. He shared an example of a typical day. On this day they had five airplanes. One was a Hawker jet in the middle of a G check inspection. A G check is needed every 2 years. During this inspection, all the seats are removed from the airplane. The airframe is x-rayed to make sure there are no cracks or weak spots. Wean was in the process of putting it back together.

The station also has a Twin Comanche. The mechanics are installing speed modifications on it. This will make the airplane fly faster. The other three airplanes they are working on include a Mooney, a Baron, and a Cessna 414. These aircraft need annual inspections.

Airline mechanics perform annual inspections. This is when they complete big upgrades and do standard repairs.

An inspection is required every year for most aircraft.

The maintenance director makes sure each mechanic knows what to work on for the day. Wean is working on putting the Hawker jet back together. But there is still more to do at a certified repair station. Sometimes, pilots call the maintenance station with a squawk. *Squawk* is the word

pilots and mechanics use for a problem.
They bring their plane to the repair station to
be fixed. It might be something simple like
refilling oil. Or it might be something more
involved like repairing a radio, an engine,
or a landing gear problem. Working on

To make sure planes run smoothly, aircraft mechanics change the oil regularly.

these unscheduled problems is called line
maintenance. The maintenance director will
pull one of his mechanics off a project. He
will send them to fix the airplane.

"I like to do line maintenance," Wean
says. "Pilots come to me with a problem,
and I diagnose it. I might find a busted
wire or figure out if something was
misprogrammed."[5] It's always rewarding
to mechanics to fix a problem and get an
aircraft back in the air.

AIRLINE MECHANICS

Many airline mechanics work at night. This
is because most airliners are flying during
the day. Some mechanics work on routine
overnight items (RON) for an aircraft. RON
inspections are one type of inspection

required by the FAA. These inspections ensure aircraft are safe and ready to fly. When mechanics arrive at work, they get a work packet. This is a list of what they need to do. They will finish as much as they can during their working hours. The list might include changing engine oil and checking for any leaks. It can include checking the aircraft for bird strikes or other damage. Mechanics might also check the tires and the brakes.

Elena Gonzalez sometimes works at night. She works in a hangar for American Airlines. Her typical 10-hour shift lasts from 9:00 p.m. to 7:00 a.m. She does maintenance on out-of-service issues. These are problems that happen again and again. Her job is to figure out why the same

Mechanics have a list of standard maintenance items they check whenever they inspect an airplane.

issues keep happening. She reads all the reports in the maintenance computer. Then she has to find the cause of the problem. Gonzalez enjoys troubleshooting these difficult issues. "I have to be able to figure out how to fix it,"[6] she says.

Other airline mechanics do line maintenance. This means they work

on aircraft as they arrive at the gates.
Sometimes a seatback gets stuck or an
overhead light goes out. The mechanics try
to fix the problem.

Sometimes a mechanic doesn't want
to delay a flight to fix a small problem.
Issues like a broken coffee maker or stuck
passenger seat don't affect the safety of the
flight. Mechanics can schedule a time to fix
these things later.

Be Careful

Aircraft mechanics have to be very careful as they
work. They must stay clear of moving aircraft.
And they need to stay away from propellers and
jet engines that are running. The suction from
a jet engine is very powerful. It can suck up
baggage or people who are too close.

DIFFERENT WORKDAYS

An aircraft mechanic's workday depends on where they work. Aircraft mechanics at smaller repair stations might work mostly during the day. Aircraft mechanics at airlines work at night as well. The airlines need mechanics 24 hours a day. But airline mechanics can trade shifts to change their schedules. They can also work two shifts in a row to earn more money. Aircraft mechanics who work at helicopter or airplane tour operations are scheduled as needed.

Todd Wean once worked for an avionics company that sent him to Ukraine and Russia. He worked on the helicopters that were transporting food for the World Food Programme. Norman Mello spent

Aircraft mechanics work day and night to
maintain planes.

2 years working for a large mining company. They used aircraft operators from around the world. Mello did safety checks on aircraft operations in South Korea, Canada, and various countries in Africa. He checked their maintenance computers. Mello made sure they were doing the proper inspections. He made sure they replaced parts before they failed. He checked to see that the parts were approved for aircraft use. Mello also confirmed they used all the correct safety procedures. These are only a few of the many jobs for aircraft mechanics.

CHAPTER FOUR

WHAT IS THE FUTURE FOR AIRCRAFT MECHANICS?

The demand for aircraft mechanics is sky high. In 2023, the aviation industry was short by 12,000 to 18,000 mechanics. About 35 percent of working mechanics were older than 55. They were getting close to retiring.

The number of mechanics in training is low. It's at least 20 percent below the amount needed to fill upcoming

The need for aircraft mechanics is on the rise. Those with this in-demand skill set will have many job opportunities.

Mechanics must be ready to inspect and repair
commercial planes as soon as they return from a flight.

job openings. In the 10 years from 2022 to 2032, employment for aircraft mechanics is expected to increase about 4 percent per year. That's about the average for most job categories. But there is already a shortage. There are about 12,800 job openings each year. Many of these are from workers who are transferring to a different field or retiring. Mechanics who have an A&P certificate should have no problem getting a job.

PAY

Aircraft mechanics earn more than most workers. The median pay is $70,740 per year. That means half of aircraft mechanics make more than that amount. The median pay for workers in general is $46,310.

Aircraft mechanics make a median income of $24,430 per year more than that.

New airline agreements are driving mechanics' wages even higher. The most recent pay scales now top out at more than $70 per hour. Aircraft mechanics earning that wage will make more than $145,000 per year. This does not include the medical and retirement benefits that the airlines provide. Airline employees also fly for free on flights with available seats.

GREAT OPPORTUNITY

For students graduating from high school, becoming an aircraft mechanic is a great opportunity. It is also a good opportunity for people who want to change jobs. The shortage of aircraft mechanics means companies are offering higher pay to fill these jobs. Airlines are also creating programs to train new mechanics. They are offering financial help for students earning an A&P certificate. Some airlines are paying all the tuition and testing fees. They offer a job immediately upon graduation.

High school graduates who like problem solving and working with their hands can do well as aircraft mechanics.

Students who complete these programs normally work for the company that paid the tuition. Other fully paid scholarships are also available.

Even for students who don't get scholarships, it can be worth it. A full A&P program can be completed in about 24 months at a cost of $32,000. Most aircraft mechanics will quickly earn this money back after taking a job.

THE WORKFORCE

Anyone who passes the FAA tests can become an aircraft mechanic. About 55 percent of aircraft mechanics are white. Hispanic or Latino mechanics make up 23 percent. About 10 percent of mechanics are Black and 7 percent

AIRCRAFT MECHANIC DEMOGRAPHICS

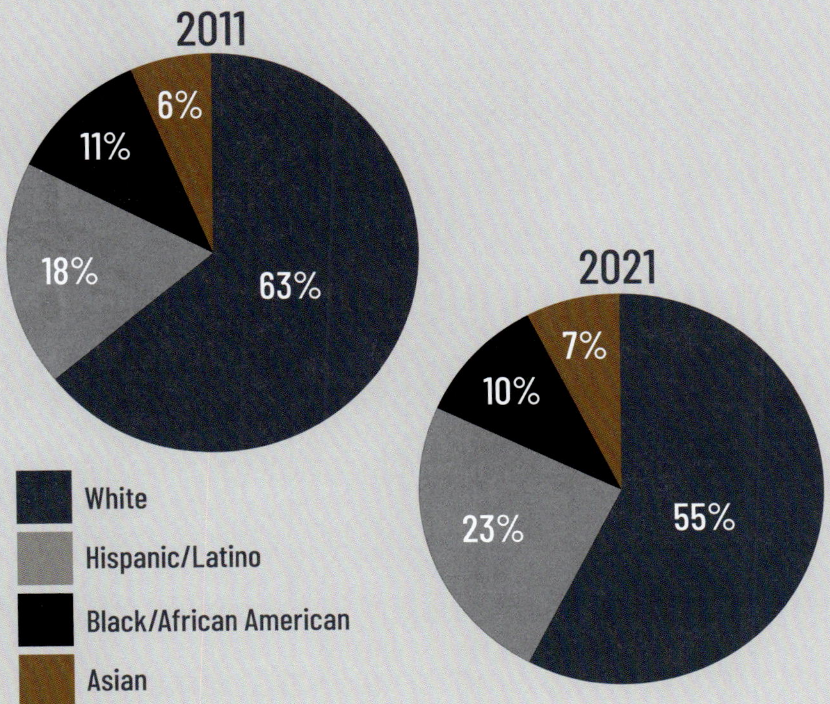

Source: "Aircraft Mechanic Demographics and Statistics in the US: Aircraft Demographics by Race," Zippia, Updated December 8, 2023. www.zippia.com.

The field of aircraft repair and maintenance grew more diverse between 2011 and 2021 as more Latino mechanics joined the ranks.

are Asian. Two percent of aircraft mechanics list themselves as part of the LGBTQ community.

Women remain underrepresented in this field. Only 7 percent of aircraft mechanics

are women. And women on average earn
11 percent less than men do.

CHANGING TECHNOLOGY

Technology is changing the way aircraft
mechanics work. New technologies in
aviation maintenance include virtual reality
(VR), augmented reality (AR), artificial
intelligence (AI), and the use of robots.

VR headsets are used to train aircraft
mechanics. They help students learn how
to remove and install airplane parts. VR
training allows them to practice on different
airplanes and systems. They can virtually fix
many kinds of problems.

AR allows instructions to be overlaid on
an actual aircraft. This means a student
wearing AR glasses could more easily find

Augmented reality allows mechanics to learn the location of different aircraft parts as they work on the engine.

what needs to be fixed. The graphics would show which panels to open or which parts to remove. AR could also show aircraft manuals and other written instructions.

AI is being used more often in aircraft maintenance. Many airplanes have computers that monitor their systems. The information gathered helps mechanics fix problems. AI also collects maintenance data from thousands of airplanes. AI systems send this data to a computer. It figures out what parts may break soon. Mechanics are able to replace parts before they fail.

Robots are used to inspect big airliners. Drones can be programmed to do the job in less time. They can fly around the aircraft and take up-close videos for mechanics to review. Crawling robots with cameras attached are also used to do inspections.

These new technologies make aircraft maintenance an exciting field. This is

3D Printers

Some aircraft parts are hard to find and take a long time to arrive. With 3D printers, these parts can be made quickly. Printed parts are exactly like the original parts. Mechanics do not have to wait for a part to arrive.

Robots complete inspections on aircraft, allowing mechanics to focus on making repairs.

especially true for mechanics who like

to learn new things. "Having an A&P is

like having a license to learn," says Elena

Gonzalez. "Aircraft change and update all

the time. You can work on different things,

from airplanes to rockets. The sky is truly

the limit as a mechanic."[7]

GLOSSARY

aircraft servicing

tasks such as inspections, maintenance, and repairs

antique aircraft

aircraft that are more than 50 years old

avionics

electronic devices on aircraft such as the radio, radar, and display screens

diagnose

to figure out what the problem is

hangar

a shelter used to store and repair aircraft

pressurization valve

a part that helps keep the correct amount of air pressure in an aircraft

radar

a device used to detect bad weather, aircraft, and other obstacles

troubleshoot

to study a problem and come up with ways to solve it

welding

using heat to connect or bond separate pieces of metal together

SOURCE NOTES

INTRODUCTION: AN IMPORTANT JOB

1. Elena Gonzalez, Personal interview, September 11, 2023.

CHAPTER ONE: WHAT DOES AN AIRCRAFT MECHANIC DO?

2. Norman Mello, Personal interview, August 18, 2023.

CHAPTER TWO: WHAT TRAINING DO AIRCRAFT MECHANICS NEED?

3. Jason Yoder, Personal interview, September 9, 2023.

CHAPTER THREE: WHAT IS LIFE LIKE AS AN AIRCRAFT MECHANIC?

4. Todd Wean, Personal interview, September 12, 2023.

5. Todd Wean, Personal interview, September 12, 2023.

6. Elena Gonzalez, Personal interview, September 11, 2023.

CHAPTER FOUR: WHAT IS THE FUTURE FOR AIRCRAFT MECHANICS?

7. Elena Gonzalez, Personal interview, September 11, 2023.

FOR FURTHER RESEARCH

BOOKS

Ib Larsen, *Become an Auto Mechanic*. San Diego, CA: BrightPoint Press, 2025.

David Macaulay, *The Way Things Work Now*. New York: Clarion Books, 2023.

Pamela McCauley, *Engineering for Teens*. New York: Rockridge Press, 2021.

INTERNET SOURCES

"7 Different Types of Helicopter Engines," *Aero Corner*, 2023. www.aerocorner.com.

Mike Ojo, "How to Build Your Own Airplane—From Cockpit to Parachute," *Popular Mechanics*, March 18, 2020. www.popularmechanics.com.

Dr. Robert J. Shaw, "How Does a Jet Engine Work?," *NASA*, May 13, 2021. www.grc.nasa.gov.

WEBSITES

AviNation
www.avinationusa.com

AviNation includes a library of videos about young adults in aviation.

Federal Aviation Administration (FAA)
www.faa.gov/education/students

The Federal Aviation Administration website has information about aviation careers for teens. It also has educational opportunities for all ages.

Pearl Harbor Aviation Museum
www.pearlharboraviationmuseum.org

The Pearl Harbor Aviation Museum includes videos and podcasts about becoming an aircraft mechanic. The site also offers scholarship opportunities.

INDEX

IMAGE CREDITS

Mike Downs is the author of more than thirty books for young people. He loves writing books that young people are excited to read. Mike has written fiction (fantasy, memoir, and poetry) and nonfiction (geography, aerospace, and science). A couple of his books are *The Flying Man: Otto Lilienthal, The World's First Pilot* and *A Treasure of Measures*.